D1112333

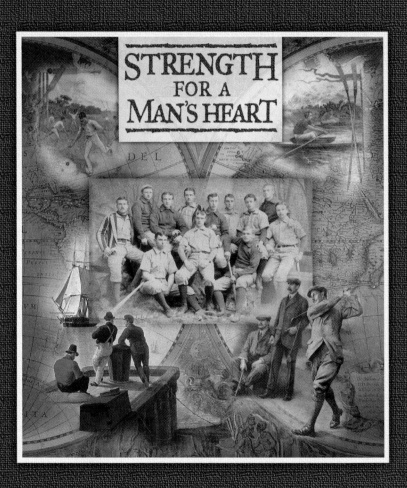

STRENGTH
FOR A
MAN'S HEART

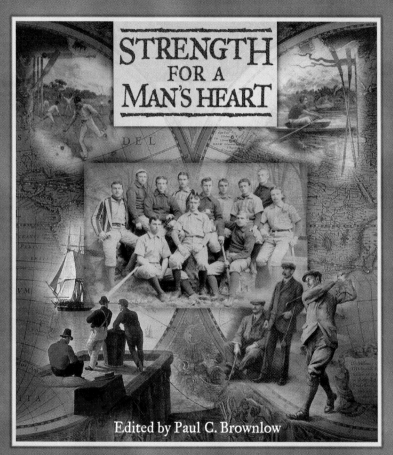

STRENGTH
FOR A
MAN'S HEART

Edited by Paul C. Brownlow

Brownlow
Brownlow Publishing Company, Inc.

Those who turn back know only the ordeal,
but they who persevere remember the adventure.

— MILO L. ARNOLD

———

To character and success, two things,
contradictory as they may seem, must go together—
humble dependence and manly independence;
humble dependence on God and manly reliance on self.

— WILLIAM WORDSWORTH

———

Hold yourself responsible for a higher standard
than anyone else expects of you.
Never excuse yourself.

— HENRY WARD BEECHER

Thank God every morning when you get up
that you have something to do which must be done,
whether you like it or not. Being forced to work,
and forced to do your best, will breed in you temperance,
self-control, diligence, strength of will, content,
and a hundred other virtues which the idle never know.

— CHARLES KINGSLEY

No man is worth his salt who is not ready
at all times to risk his body, to risk his well-being,
to risk his life, in a great cause.

— THEODORE ROOSEVELT

The most important thing in life is to live your life
for something more important than your life.

— ANONYMOUS

Baseball is
90 percent mental.
The other half is physical.

— YOGI BERRA

He is a wise man who does
not grieve for the things
which he has not, but rejoices
for those which he has.

— EPICTETUS

Things could be worse.
Suppose our errors were counted
and published everyday
like those of a baseball player.

Many men go fishing their entire lives
without knowing it is not fish
they are after.

— HENRY DAVID THOREAU

———————

The charm of fishing is that it is the pursuit
of what is elusive but obtainable,
a perpetual series of occasions for hope.

— JOHN BUCHAN

———————

Govern a family as you would
cook small fish—very gently.

— CHINESE PROVERB

How can a young man keep his way pure?

By living according to your word.

I seek you with all my heart;

do not let me stray from your commands.

— Psalm 119:9, 10

If you are not guided by God,

you will be guided by someone

or something else.

— Eric Liddell

A great man shows his greatness

by the way he treats little men.

— Thomas Carlyle

John   Tom

THE FIRE
OF AMBITION

The successful man
has ambition:
Before an engine
has any power,
it must have a fire
under the boilers.
Ambition was the fire
that stirred Edison, Lindbergh,
and other successful men
who have been
more interested in
achievement than in
public applause.

— A. B. ZU TAVERN

DAILY CHOICES

Character is distilled out of our
daily confrontation with temptation,
out of our regular response to the call of duty.
It is formed as we learn to cherish principles
and to submit to self-discipline.
Character is the sum total of all the little decisions,
the small deeds, the daily reactions to
the choices that confront us.
Character is not obtained instantly.
We have to mold and hammer
and forge ourselves into character.
It is a distant goal to which there is no shortcut.

— SIDNEY GREENBERG

One thought
driven home
is better than three
left on base.

— JAMES LITER

Progress always
involves risk;
you can't steal second base
and keep your foot on first.

— ANONYMOUS

Cheerfulness is the great lubricant of the wheels of life.
It lightens labor, diminishes difficulties,
and mitigates misfortunes. Cheerfulness gives a
creative power which the pessimist never possesses.
A sunny, hopeful, optimistic disposition sweetens life,
lightens its inevitable drudgery,
and eases the jolts along the road.

— COUNCILLOR

He is happiest, be he king or peasant,
who finds peace in his home.

— JOHANN WOLFGANG VON GOETHE

We have not inherited the earth from our fathers,
we are borrowing it from our children.

— NATIVE AMERICAN PROVERB

A ship in harbor is safe,
but that is not what
ships are built for.

— John Shedd

———————

Ideals are like stars:
you will not succeed
in touching them
with your hands,
but like the seafaring man
on the desert of waters,
you choose them
as your guides,
and following them
you reach your destiny.

— Carl Schurz

Golf is 20 percent mechanics and technique.
The other 80 percent is philosophy, humor,
tragedy, romance, melodrama, companionship,
camaraderie, cussedness, and conversation.

— GRANTLAND RICE

———————

Sign on a Scottish golf course:
"Members will refrain from picking up
lost golf balls until they stop rolling."

———————

In golf as in life it's the follow-through
that makes the difference.

— ANONYMOUS

Angling may be said to be so like mathematics
that it can never be fully learned.

— Izaak Walton, *The Compleat Angler*

There are as good fish in the sea as ever came out of it.

— English Proverb

Fear not that thy life shall come to an end,
but rather fear that it shall never have a beginning.

— John Henry Newman

It's good to have money and the things
that money can buy, but it's good, too,
to check up once in a while and make sure
you haven't lost the things that money can't buy.

— George Horace Lorimer

STRENGTH OF CHARACTER

Strength of character means strong feelings, and
strong command over them. This is where foresight,
judgment, and will-power unite to form the most
vital and important cement of a strong personality.
To subordinate the lower nature to the higher, to be
able to forego a present pleasure for a greater future good,
is a distinguishing mark of the highest type of character.
Self-denial is essential to manhood; for,
to make one's life count, demands sacrifice.

— Councillor

———————————

The more I study nature,
the more I am amazed at the Creator.

— Louis Pasteur

SOMETHING MORE

Just do what you can. It's not enough merely to exist.
It's not enough to say, "I'm earning enough to live and
support my family. I do my work well. I'm a good father.
I'm a good husband." That's all very well. But you
must do something more. Seek always to do some good,
somewhere. Every man has to seek in his own way to make
his own self more noble and to realize his own true worth.

You must give some time to your fellowman.
Even if it's a little thing, do something for those who have
need of help, something for which you get no pay
but the privilege of doing it. For remember, you don't live
in a world all your own. Your brothers are here, too.

— ALBERT SCHWEITZER

Success is to be measured not so much by the position that
one has reached in life as by the obstacles which he has overcome.

— BOOKER T. WASHINGTON

A truly spiritual man's creed
is not live and let live,
but live and help live.

— ROGER BABSON

I want to be thoroughly used up when I die,
for the harder I work, the more I live.
Life is no brief candle for me.
It is a sort of splendid torch which
I have got hold of for a moment,
and I want to make it burn as brightly
as possible before handing it on
to future generations.

— GEORGE BERNARD SHAW

We are all in the same boat in a stormy sea,
and we owe each other a terrible loyalty.

— G. K. Chesterton

The Lord will either calm your storm
or allow it to rage while He calms you.

— Anonymous

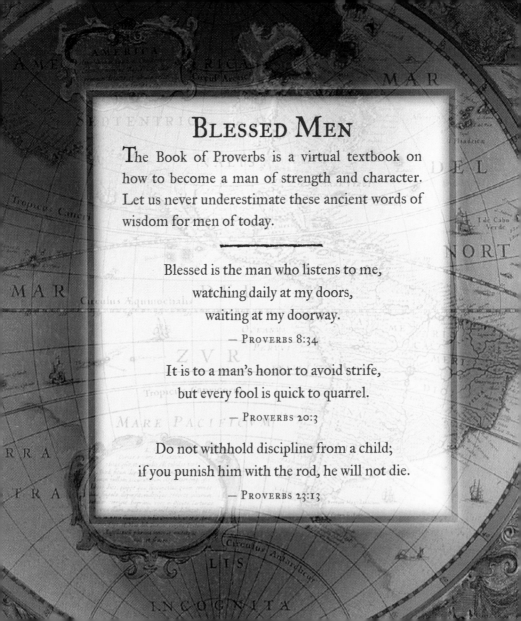

Blessed Men

The Book of Proverbs is a virtual textbook on how to become a man of strength and character. Let us never underestimate these ancient words of wisdom for men of today.

———————

Blessed is the man who listens to me,
watching daily at my doors,
waiting at my doorway.

— Proverbs 8:34

It is to a man's honor to avoid strife,
but every fool is quick to quarrel.

— Proverbs 20:3

Do not withhold discipline from a child;
if you punish him with the rod, he will not die.

— Proverbs 23:13

Do not wear yourself out to get rich;
have the wisdom to show restraint.
Cast but a glance at riches, and they are gone.

— Proverbs 23:4, 5

Do not love sleep or you will grow poor;
stay awake and you will have food to spare.

— Proverbs 20:13

Many are the plans in a man's heart,
but it is the Lord's purpose that prevails.

— Proverbs 19:21

A greedy man brings trouble to his family.

— Proverbs 15:27

A hot-tempered man must pay the penalty;
if you rescue him, you will have to do it again.

— Proverbs 19:19

A faithful man will be richly blessed.

— PROVERBS 28:20

Like a city whose walls are broken down
is a man who lacks self-control.

— PROVERBS 25:28

Do not envy wicked men,
do not desire their company.

— PROVERBS 24:1

Commit to the Lord whatever you do,
and your plans will succeed.

— PROVERBS 16:3

Blessed is the man who finds wisdom,
the man who gains understanding.

— PROVERBS 3:13

A simple man believes anything,
but a prudent man gives thought to his steps.

— PROVERBS 14:15

A generous man will prosper;
he who refreshes others will himself be refreshed.

— PROVERBS 11:25

May you rejoice in the wife of your youth;
may you ever be captivated by her love.

— PROVERBS 5:18, 19

An anxious heart weighs a man down,
but a kind word cheers him up.

— PROVERBS 12:25

Lazy hands make a man poor,
but diligent hands bring wealth.

— PROVERBS 10:4

You're a man, you've seen the world—
The beauty and the wonder and the power,
The shape of things, their colors, lights, and shades,
Changes, surprises—and God made it all!

— ROBERT BROWNING

Every man dies, but not every man lives.

— WILLIAM WALLACE

Anyone who proposes to do good must not
expect people to roll stones out of his way,
but must accept his lot calmly if they even roll
a few more on it. A strength which becomes clearer
and stronger through experiences of such obstacles
is the only strength that can conquer them.
Resistance is only a waste of strength.

— ALBERT SCHWEITZER

A Relish for the Game

Wherein do the charms of this game lie, that captivate youth, and retain their hold till far on in life? It is a fine, open-air, athletic exercise, not violent, but bringing into play nearly all the muscles of the body, with exercise that can be continued for hours.

It is a game of skill, needing mind and thought and judgment, as well as a cunning hand. It is also a social game, where one may go out with one friend or with three, as the case may be, and enjoy mutual exchange, mingled with an excitement which is very pleasing.

The game of golf never palls or grows stale, as morning by morning the players appear at the teeing-ground with as keen a relish as if they had not seen a club for a month. Nor is it only while the game lasts that its zest is felt. How the player loves to recall the strokes and other incidents of the match, so that it is often played over again next morning while still in bed!

— James Balfour

You are already of consequence in the world
if you are known as a man of strict integrity.
If you can be absolutely relied upon;
if when you say a thing is so, it is so;
if when you say you will do a thing,
you do it; then you carry with you
a passport to universal esteem.

— GRENVILLE KLEISER

A great man is a man who lives great principles.
The greatest men the world has ever known
were criticized, often bitterly, but they
didn't let themselves get discouraged.
And this is one of the secrets of their greatness.

— ANONYMOUS

Far better it is to dare mighty things,
to win glorious triumphs even though
checkered by failures, than to rank
with those poor spirits who neither
enjoy much nor suffer much
because they live in the gray twilight
that knows not victory or defeat.

— THEODORE ROOSEVELT

How good and pleasant it is
when brothers dwell together in unity.

— PSALM 113:1

When we serve, we rule;
When we surrender ourselves,
we are victors.

— JOHN HENRY NEWMAN

SUCCESSFUL MEN

The successful man cooperates:

We live in an age of cooperation when men

succeed as they work together—team-work.

The organization that cannot cooperate cannot succeed.

In the future, it will be difficult for any

employee to stay on the payroll very long who

is unable to mix agreeably with his co-workers.

One of the qualities of increasing importance

that makes for success is the ability

to cooperate with other people.

— A. B. Zu Tavern

God did not write solo parts for very many of us.
He expects us to be participants in the great symphony of life.

— Donald Tippett

THE GAME OF LIFE

Our business in life is not to get ahead of other people,

but to get ahead of ourselves. To break our own record,

to outstrip our yesterdays by todays, to bear our trials

more beautifully than we ever dreamed we could,

to whip the tempter inside and out as we never

whipped him before, to give as we never have given,

to do our work with more force and a finer finish

than ever—this is the true ideal—to get ahead of ourselves.

To beat someone else in a game, or to be beaten,

may mean much or little. To beat our own game

means a great deal. Whether we win or not,

we are playing better than we ever did before, and

that's the point after all—to play a better game of life.

PONY POST

COVERED WAGON

COVERED WAGON

Do not follow where the path may lead.
Go instead where there is no path, and leave a trail.

— Anonymous

———————

It's a wise man who profits by his own experiences,

but it's a good deal wiser one

who lets the rattlesnake bite the other fellow.

— Josh Billings

THE STUFF OF LIFE

We cannot tell what may happen to us

in the strange medley of life.

But we can decide what happens in us —

how we can take it, what we do with it —

and that is what really counts in the end.

How to take the raw stuff of life and make it

a thing of worth and beauty — that is the test of living.

Life is an adventure of faith,

if we are to be victors over it, not victims of it.

My great concern is not whether God is on our side,
my great concern is to be on God's side.

— ABRAHAM LINCOLN

A New Beginning

Every morning is a fresh beginning.

Every day is the world made new.

Today is a new day.

Today is my world made new.

I have lived all my life up to this moment,

to come to this day.

This moment — this day — is as good

as any moment in all eternity.

I shall make of this day — a heaven on earth.

This is my day of opportunity.

— DAN CUSTER

A. Moore ?   S. Hall ?   J.P. Hardwick P.   M. Brown P.   K.H. Fitz
        A.E. Scott   Asst. Finbeck   J.A. Topp   Asst. J. Mug
                                      McSoles   Sur

Noble Souls

Courage consists not in
hazarding without fear,
but being resolutely
minded in a just cause.
The brave man is not
he who feels no fear, for that
were stupid and irrational,
but he whose noble soul
subdues its fear, and bravely
dares the danger
nature shrinks from.

— Ferrold

The world is divided into people who do things
and people who get the credit; try to belong
to the first class—there's far less competition.

— Dwight Whitney Morrow

The golden age only comes to men
when they have forgotten gold.

— G. K. Chesterton

The world and its desires pass away,
but the man who does the will of God lives forever.

— 1 John 2:17

Whatever we see, wherever we look,

whether we recognize it as true or not,

we cannot touch or handle the things

of earth and not, in that very moment,

be confronted with the sacraments of heaven.

— C. A. Coulson

———————

To every man there comes in his lifetime

that special moment when he is

figuratively tapped on the shoulder and

offered that chance to do a very special thing,

unique to him and fitted to his talents.

— Winston Churchill

GREAT DREAMS

We grow great by dreams. All big men are dreamers.

They see things in the soft haze of a spring day

or in the red fire of a long winter's evening.

Some of us let these great dreams die,

but others nourish and protect them;

nurse them through bad days till they

bring them to the sunshine and light

which comes always to those who hope

that their dreams will come true.

— WOODROW WILSON